A Book of Poems

The Order of Creation

by

Sarah Whiteley

Published by 2nd Tier Publishing
Wimberley, Texas, USA
© 2015 All rights reserved

First published by Sarah Whiteley
© 2011 All rights reserved

Original book design by Karen Messer
Design edited by Nikos Rovakis

Cover Art by Sarah Whiteley, Jeraldene Lovell-Cole & Karen Messer
Edited by Niamh Carey
Author Photo by Shiila Safer

Whiteley, Sarah
The Order of Creation

ISBN: 978-0-9862290-3-9

To Life ~ Zoi ~ ζωή

CREATING THE ORDER OF CREATION

The Order of Creation chronicles a
pathway of living life through a
perspective of wholeness expressed by
the practice of conscious, intentional
evolution and sourced from, and
inspired by, fields of Living Wholeness
and Axladitsa Avatakia, Greece.

⌒

I have travelled the arc of the moon with you.
The waxing, the waning,
The dark side, the full bloom,
Shadows and mystery,
Brilliance, deep feminine,
Aspects that pave the skies I now walk.

The Arc of the Moon
p 32

If I thanked all the beings within this creation,
I would start right from life's source
And end with infinity.

Yet between these environs,
Dear ones gifted presence, passion, generosity,
Pure energy and deep heart.

So please meet the beauties who poured forth their magic.
I deeply thank each one
For gifting their gift.

⌒⟩

Dear Life – how I thank you,
For wholeness and mystery.
The pattern: worlds of poetry,
Immense spirit, source landscape.

Dear Land – Axladitsa.
Roots stretched out through acres,
Ancientness awakened,
Beckoning the new.

⌒⟩

Dear Maria mou – blessèd one.
Unconditional love's teacher,
Majestic path-weaver,
Light-beam in flight.

Dear Vanessa - bright artist.
Wonderment's pure knowing
Spanning life-times of meaning
Flowing age after age.

Dear Karen – truth's seer.
Life's sweetness and beauty,
Elegance of heart space,
Bountiful and paced.

Dear Kamyar - sweet mystic.
Life's resonance embodied,
Unity's step forward,
Presence held each day.

Dear Karen - Sophia's guardian.
Generous depth reader,
Re-patterning the brightness,
Witnessing the work.

Dear Jeraldene - source essence.
Cradling life's magic,
Lighter of pathways,
Intuition's deep song.

Dear Clive – proud watcher.
Ground holder, protector.
Gifting soul's wisdom with
Simplicity and play.

Dear Linda – space holder.
Patient, wise doula,
Joy weaver, ground-speaker,
Truth's partner every way.

Dear Yitzhak – dear elder.
Friend and protector,
Generous, insightful,
Presence constant, held dear.

Dear Freddie - loyal watcher.
Playmate and walk-guider,
Kairos' time-keeper,
Bliss deep every day.

Dear Family – the Whiteleys.
Ann, Jonathan, Ginia, Mark.
Root container of journeying,
Artist's path, our way.

Index

Unless

Unless we engage our authentic selves,
We cannot live the future now.

Unless we engage our fullness,
We cannot take the leap individually and call in collectively.

Unless we tremble collectively,
We cannot presence the new.

Unless we take a leap together,
We cannot access and live the next level of our humanity.

Unless we are willing to hold the space open long enough for our
Collective clarity to emerge,
We cannot shift our systems and behaviour for the better.

Unless we fuse the streams of practice and inquiry,
We cannot see what else is possible and be prepared to meet our chaos.

Unless we acknowledge our collective identity,
We cannot co-create our real work.

Unless we understand our complicatedness,
We cannot find the simplicity of the next elegant step.

Unless we share our new insights immediately,
We do not serve evolution.

Unless we burn for something real,
We will not live our destiny.

Unless we live through our collective identity,
We cannot become whole.

Cycles of Identity

Shifts in time,
Episodes of life
Call for expression
Of gifts held dormant.

Not quite time
To let them loose,
So patiently waiting
In the wings

Until curtain call.
The moment is here,
Of life saying
Now you are on!

Newness is pregnant,
The gifts are ripened
And ready to flow
Beyond the boundaries.

Time to weave them
Into the web
Of service and meaning.
Gifts to ground

Feeding the growth
Until time signals
The next moment
Of new identity

Flowing from the centre.
Again the shift:
Time calling all
To the next level.

The Medicine Woman and the Wise Woman

They are here!

Both of them

Standing strong

Together, yet separate

In their own ground

In their own work

In service

Of the community.

Calling in the others:

The warriors,

The builders,

The inspirers

And creators of the new.

Those who are ready to respond with

Ground, dignity and strength.

There is no room for those who shy away

From the work,

From the world,

Calling for change:

For community,

For learning,

For integrity,

For wholeness.

It is time to share the gifts

In service of the whole,

In service of life,

For nothing else is enough.

The time has come

To gather,

To commit,

To say yes,

And to act.

Lost

Have you ever been lost

In blind panic,
Bereft of all reference points,
Shrouded in mist
Terrified to your core?

Have you ever been lost

In the gifts of love of
Another
To find you have lost
Connection to self?

Have you ever been lost
And scurried
Here and there
Frantic to find known places
A voice, a smile?

Have you ever been lost

And wandered in the dark
Wondering if life and light
Will ever touch your soul
And sooth the spirit?

Have you ever been lost,

Travelled through landscapes
Where all is a blur
And time has forgotten to call
You friend?

Have you ever been lost,

Yet music
A lover
A landmark
A memory
A prayer
A phone call
A smile

Has called you home?

Fit for a Planet

Who makes the blue prints for the new world:

Who are the draftsmen, the architects,

the artists, the visionaries?

Look! There they are!

Stooped over the drawing board,

slide rule and pencil in hand.

Tricky business making blue prints,

Needed in scale and stature,

The size of a planet.

Still, someone's got to do it,

Got to start

Drawing the base-lines, scoping possibility.

Otherwise, we stay with the same model,

The same ground plan,

The same design.

But the design is shifting,

To house the newness calling

To be loved and lived into being.

So the draftsmen, the architects and the others

Stoop studiously late into the night,

Crafting the ground plan

Fit for a planet.

The Wild Nature

How much do we love the wild nature?
The earthy,
The fiery,
The passionate one.

How much do we revere the wild nature,
Honour the cycles
Of rise and fall?
So real, essence trembles.

How much do we allow the wild nature to
really show up?
Could we handle the power,
Stand tall, side by side?

How much do we fear the wild nature?
Would our heart ease in awe
Or would fear rise in our throat
Making us shrink and shadow?

How much do we cultivate the wild nature?
Calling its voice,
Letting it roam,
Without question.

How much do we capture the wild nature?
Trimming wings and tails,
The sensory organs
Of the soul.

How much do we recognise the wild nature?
Or do we walk past
With a polite nod,
Without thought or recognition?

How much do we long for the wild nature?
Wish for the embrace
To take us home
To peaceful lands.

How much have we missed the wild nature?
Or have we dissed it?
Resisted it?
Shame on you.

Boom!

The system shift is on!
In the conversations
In the hearts
In the eyes
In the hands
Of those who care
To dare
To face
Full frontal
The need for change

To rearrange the matrix
So the basics
And the next level
Can find their place
Of balance
And service
To turn it around
Like a liner on course
Yet the course has changed
And the movement is still moving

The pilot boats are out
With thick ropes
And strong shouts
To bring this liner to rest
So the new
The one who
Knows it's time
Is now!
Time to anchor
The banter that this cannot be done

'Cos BOOM
The river has claimed its course
And the source that inspires
The route is now clear.

The Stake in the Ground

There once was a stake in the ground
  That irked our dear neighbour profound.
    They argued the case,
     It was not our place,
      To legally map truth all around.

    But this was our stake so to claim,
     We had papers to prove its clear gain,
      But things got unclear,
       So truth took a steer
        To invite law to come and take rein.

     Fact is these events are unfolding,
      Can't say it isn't foreboding,
       Our ground is intact,
        And stronger in fact,
        For wholeness is part of the holding.

     And, friends if you feel so inclined,
      To pass on clear thought and good chime,
       That this place is tended,
        With hearts strong and mended,
        And the land once again is aligned.

     I know that many of us choose
      To use 'stake' as a metaphor and muse.
       It really is clear,
        Integrity is dear,
        A significant part of its fuse.

When the Well runs Bone Dry

What do we do
When the well runs bone dry
On this small land
And natural subsystem?
Do we just call for more
To be brought in from town,
From the neighbouring,
Overflowing
Mainstream

That uses the water
To cool the hot concrete
Just as the taverna gets toasty?
It's not about being
Too fundamental,
Yet it raises big questions in me.
And so here we are,
Sensing the movement
Of how to release from the drought.

And is this the answer
To assume that we can
Simply add a huge wave to the mix?
It seems so bizarre
To have worked and been mindful
To then simply pick up the phone.
But perhaps our best efforts
Are done just for now;
Simply stop and notice the tensions.

Yet wisdom speaks loudly
That calling for more
Is not the step I should take.
I just want to feel,
To feel in my bones,
That our Earth
May not have a back-up.
And it is up to us
To watch with compassion
That we are the ones who must change.

As Right in at this moment
Of So many people in the world
Do not have another mains-system
Yet others some of us use
Our Earth like it's full
Of all that we want in our minds
But this is not true
As we think we have more
And Yet our resources must host
All of us.

Message from the Monk's Cave

Fear not the separation,

Of a life lived by others.

This one is for you,

For now.

Messages flow to a life

That is brim-filled

With joy and friendship,

Gatherings and words.

All well and good.

This too brings wisdom,

Yet there is another language

That becomes the soul,

One that hears life's impulse,

Aloneness being the way,

A singular path,

That calls in a moment.

A moment in nature,

Simple and true,

That holds the promise

Of life meeting life.

When questions and answers

With silence flow forth

And the wind and the pathway

Being the company you keep.

So reside in the cave with the monk

For a while,

It is calling in stillness,

Beckoning, beckoning.

Snakeskin at the Doorway

You leave me today,
Dear friends and dear one,
And travel to live
Your next chapter.
And as I re-ground,
Holding that which is mine,
I see that skin
Has been shed.

In the days that we shared
And the life that we wove
Here is the sign
Of new birthing.
Yet I ask is it mine?
Is it yours? Is it ours?
Or, is it all of them
Wrapped up together?

I tend to believe
That we lived
Sacred space,
That words cannot
Capture or fathom,
But I know in my heart
That truth wove its magic
And broke open ground
In our centres.

So I now wish to mark
This precious new doorway,
That sloughed off skin
We can measure.
It is also so clear
That my love
Is most dearly
Part of the matrix
That binds us.

But we must bring our beings,
Our scars
And our visions
To bear in this
Most sacred centre.
We have many new spaces
To open in places
That our dreams
Have not even signalled.

Quake in the Distance

How does it touch me,
This quake in the distance?
Do I hold people and place
More strongly?

How does it move me,
This quake in the distance?
Does it shake my own bones
To awaken?

How does it call me,
This quake in the distance?
Does it open my heart to
Step forward?

How does it remind me,
This quake in the distance?
Do I realise that all is
Connected?

How does it bond me,
This quake in the distance,
To hold the Earth in its
Trembling?

How does it teach me,
This quake in the distance,
To witness the world's soul
In her moving?

How does it press me,
This quake in the distance,
To balance the Earth
With my stillness?

Yes,
Right
To
My
Core.

Turtle

Thankfully this time
My dog didn't disturb you,
Not lifting you up
As if you were stone,
His jaw stretched and widened,
You lumpy and silent
Like a crusty old sandwich
In a forgotten lunch box.

Thankfully, too,
Your path was unhindered
As he was tied to his lead
And simply walked by,
Not burying you as last year
Like a prized bone,
Only found by a friend
Who tracked his misdeed.

And so, since you walked on,
What is your meaning
To me on my pathway?
This day of thick cloud
Shrouding the sunlight
And cooling the breeze,
A day of the first soup
To warm me right
through.

This morning it was wild boar
And now it is you dear
That I see on my walkway
The very same day.

All precious companions
In human-less spaces
I return to the kitchen
And settle, to hear

Turtle – Mother Earth
The oldest of symbols,
The essence of goddess,
Eternal black soil.
Shell as protector,
Deep nurturer, volcano,
Your shield is unwavering
In the face of attack.

A teacher of grounding,
Slow paced
With compassion,
Focussed to complete
Whatever the end.
Don't push the river,
Time will just plod by,
It's a way that has sweetness,
So give it a try.

Harvest when ready,
Until then, don't worry,
Life is unfolding
In ways still unknown.
Protect simple newness
Hare's rush - why hurry?
Remember the ally
Of dear Mother Earth.

Immeasurable Beauty

I don't think I will tire
Of the view of the Aegean,
The immeasurable beauty
That greets me each day.

Her depth and her presence,
Her majesty and elegance
Are simply the qualities that
Speak of her blue.

Sometimes with storm clouds,
Strong blown to white caps,
A windsurfers paradise,
A fisherman's friend.

Other times unruffled,
Mirrored in stillness,
Serene in her knowing,
Profound to her depth.

So again I am greeted
By her immeasurable beauty,
Red sunned and light struck,
In early morning light.

The Feta Rap

What is better
Than feta
In a bowl?

I knows it 'cos
I chose it.

The peppers,
All fired and
Toasted,
Know it too.

It's local, see,
It's all Greek to me,
From sheep

And the deep
Red soil of home.

So cheer it up,
Feta's here!

Like a caped
Crusader
Made ta
Make you siesta

All

After

Noon.

Sunrise in my Rear-view Mirror

Stunning sunrise in my rearview mirror.
A clear signal of wheels heading west.
A boon for my waking soul
As the stars begin to take their rest.

Connection to home-place
Like a gossamer thread
Spinning me forward
To weave a new web.

A smile curls my mouth
As your face greets mine,
Red, fiery, luscious,
Stroking sleepless temples,

Inspiring my journey,
Warming my back,
Calling me forth,
Returning me home.

Wait! Now you are ahead!
Moving east and south,
Lighting a speedy journey
Into grey-toned mountains.

Landscape changes,
More habitation.
Emptiness, plains,
Bound south, west…airplanes.

Thirty degrees your warmth tells me,
As I step lightly forward
Into day's journey.
Here you will stay, there I will go!

Speaking of Wholeness

In twenty-three hours, an array of colour-threads
On a life-loom of wholeness, creating a weave.

Misunderstandings, grounding, make-ups and tears,
Luscious lunch, home-cooked, farewells and kisses.

Train ride southwards, sleeping companions,
Underground chatting, terminal divergence.

Heathrow T4, checkpoints and tourists,
Family text timing, loved ones missed.

Boarding at night time, sleeping, sleep, sleeping,
Arrival in homeland, autumn rain's sweetness,

Phone calls and emails, a sign of safe passage,
A coffee and chocolate: OK, ready to roll.

Drive in the darkness, awakening to the sun,
Six hours of sing-song, arriving at noon.

Driveway is reshaped by recent strong rainstorm,
Nature's tale of events, painted on stone.

Dogs are ecstatic, leap like on pogos,
Cats are still cooler, wishing to preen.

Down to the garden, whoa…tomatoes abundant,
Nine for the lunch pot, peppers all green.

Resting from journeying, memories rolling,
A day of life's wholeness, still one hour to go.

Silence is Often

Silence is often underrated,

Delegated to the back of the line,

A tone in its own time,

Undisturbed by the others.

Silence is often feared,

Yet revered by soul's longing,

For stillness and solitude,

Where silence meets its mate.

Silence is often embraced

And traced to the deepest corners,

Of the globe, the back-tracking

And landing into moments of peace.

Silence is often powerful punctuation

In the mainstream motion,

Of lives lived loud,

Yet waits to be invited, always.

Yet silence is often

Most welcomed in my day,

To share the tones and wonder,

That otherwise stay silent.

Silence is often deemed a solitary act,

One that asks for space to be cleared,

Yet as powerful as any,

Are the ones shared with others.

Puzzle Pieces – Building Blocks

Puzzle pieces rock
Pools diamond's
Facet threaded
Spools

Tones of magic
Impulses thrown
Dancing spirals
Shapes unknown

Construct, destruct
Find the edge
Penetrate
Name your pledge

Close the circle
Do the deed
Research business
Based on need

Name the homes
Create the frame
Masteries challenge
Partners to claim

Steward the new
Grounded in depth
Outreach café
Claims the breadth

Purpose money
Legacy's wish
Chance to action
Partnership's bliss

Choice is present
Earth's great call
Models and practice
Patterns for all

Close the journey
Of less intent
Walk the new path
Destiny sent

Balance the natures
Call the others
Align in passions
True blood brothers

Watch the weather
Hear the quake
Time to share
The shape we make

Piece the puzzle
Pool the rocks
Facet the diamond
Build the blocks.

The Arc of the Moon

I have travelled the arc of the moon with you.
The waxing, the waning,
The dark side, the full bloom.
Shadows and mystery,
Brilliance, deep feminine,
Aspects that pave the skies I now walk.

Aching Bones

Aching bones – what is your message?
Why do you hound me this way?

Aching bones – won't you rest easy?
Please allow our strong essence to play.

Aching bones – why are you speaking
In tones that are difficult to hear?

Aching bones – where are you leading,
When the path is really not clear?

Aching bones – you speak every morning,
Nagging my curiosity awake.

Aching bones – my mind is on fire
To know the response I should take.

Aching bones – I've known you from ages,
Yet your tone is increasing in scale.

Aching bones – please offer your wisdom,
In language that tells of your tale.

Aching bones – you channel of wonder,
How much you have travelled in life.

Aching bones – your wish is to honour
The mission I hold like a knife.

Aching bones – I know I must listen
To all that you know and must tell,

Aching bones – I'm listening, please trust me,
Your voice is as clear as a bell.

Aching bones – last night I wrote this
To honour the truth that you speak,

Aching bones - I wake to your mighty
Surpassed pain upon pain all this week.

Aching bones – I sense that your message
Is calling the foundations to rock,

Aching bones – implicit I trust you
To shake my whole being to talk.

Aching bones – please trust my own timing
Of forming the wisdom to tell,

Aching bones – my cells are awakened
Please join me in ringing the bell!

The River...and the River Below

Most often you're shrouded, deep in soil's structures,
Caressing and strengthening Earth's strong heartbeat,
Cooling and moistening the roots diving deep,
Soothing all life forms,
Cutting through stone.

Yet, today you are audible, like chimes of a church bell,
Calling in service of those who believe.
With such ease and grace, you move in the topside,
Elegance itself is
Weaving your hand.

In flowing formations, with droplets connecting,
Racing and gliding to rock pools in wait.
A syncopated timing, not called in by others,
Signalled by sky's love,
Opening its heart.

But sooner or later, your voice will fall silent,
As you dry up in places you'd recently been seen.
This is the rhythm you ebb and return in,
To the depths where you nurture
The timeless deep well.

How clearly you offer now the rhythms of nature

That exist at all levels, in every life form.

And the gift that you offer, is that you are our nature,

So pushing the river

Is not the true flow.

Be patient and watchful, the timing of living,

The natural tides that hold heart's strongest beat.

Trust life and be called to the topside bright river,

Or descend to the magic of

Life's unstoppable flow.

And so it was true that this cycle was over,

This very morning your voice was not here.

Your travels above ground had offered such richness,

And now it was time to

Return to the depths.

Complex Adaptive System at a Cellular Level

Today I feel Nature
At a cellular level
As one anchor changes
The whole pattern Shifts

A travel trajectory
New and unfolding
Shifts in the questions
Timing that's meant

Both Insider and Outsider
Seek Knowledge for Centre
Intuitive clear Sensing
Fact-finding with Mates

Friends offer respite
Others tend the Livestock
Conditions now needed
For newness to land

New meetings to meet in
Presence releasing
Pre-sensed responses
No longer are real

New is now Visible
Pathways have shifted
Fundamental re-frames
To let Life live in flow

Despair

Is it possible to rid the mind of despair?
On days like today it is not.

The tones of deep tiredness, misguided and fractious,
Painting all shades of the action to grey.

Is it possible to move towards hoping,
Not knowing the co-ordinates that transcend time?

Soul searching and sensing from all that is present,
Shrouding all deepest knowing in darkness.

Is it possible that life calls in awakening,
In moments when breathing is tense?

To step forward in meaning that only through seeking,
Consciousness itself holds intent.

Is it possible that these days are a gifting,
To undo and unlearn the deep patterns,

To trouble the soul, redefining the goal,
Transiting to pathways that serve?

One Son's Eclipse on a Lunar Night

Son's quality shone like a moonbeam,
Curving threads across dark night-time's sky.
Three aspects creating life's goodness,
Weaving patterns and witnessed with joy.

Mother, friend, neighbour – three beings of being,
Co-creators of lunar light magic,
Strong standing presence, deep holding,
Birthed magic that cooked in the middle.

Shining beams of brilliant bright starlight,
He, himself, moved throughout time.
Then time opened up like a firefly,
Then curled closed, like a leaf seeped in dew.

Then mystery called his name out loud,
You, my Son, are most blessèd.
His arc was complete and life witnessed,
Son's eclipse gifting lunar's night.

Ta Fota

Yesterday we celebrated Ta Fota,
The day that light honoured a king.
A light from the east, brought in threefold,
Bestowed by love's courageous blessing.

Yesterday, I met with Ta Fota,
The light too bestowed love's blessing,
Deep into a heart breaking open,
Paining from waking and growing.

Today I honour Ta Fota,
That brought simply blessings anew.
Consciousness naming new thresholds,
And lighting one journey of truth.

The Artist

The artist journeys
With all
That makes life beautiful,
Powerful, special, sacred
And brings into form
For all to see.

The artist travels
The realms
Of edge and inspiration
Drawing breath from all
That is whole
To be the now.

The artist's reality
Is being
Real time, doing as a seer,
Capturing a moment,
Life's inherent bliss,
Trusting life's gifts.

The artist is my sister
Who I love
Most dearly
Who I honour
As she walks
Her artistic life.

Possibility of Loss

A place seeped with ambiguous pathways,
Potential scenarios,
Unrequited actions.

A place filled with waves of fear;
Sadness and grief
Reminiscing love.

A place layered with erratic randomness,
Thought and emotion
Unable to rest.

Debris of the Civilised World

We search beyond the boundary,

Travelling pathways towards the village.

A neighbour suggested we look there.

Off we go,

No sign.

Were we searching in vain?

Perhaps.

Were we too late?

Maybe.

Important we still try.

⌒

Our walk home speaks of tensions,

The way forward.

Keep looking?

Keep sensing?

Keep connecting?

Keep hoping?

All are true.

⌒

On our return, I walk the streambed,
The wildest place with the biggest trees.
Badgers, foxes and wild boar travel this way.
Today I walk with one of our nine cats,
Quiet and dark, shadowed and lit,

The pace and place serene.

Stumbling, I reach a pile of trash
Remains
From previous times,
Pushed down the slope,
Wishing life to be pushed out of sight.
Now debris in this sacred space,
Civilised artefacts cluttering the Earth,
Blighting this landscape.

Winding my way up the streambed,
I call her name again.
Looking back at the debris,
I realise I have civilised her.

Afraid of the realities of local life,

Boar, hunters, cars, poison,

A kick from a neighbour.

Did she run free

To return to the wild?

⌒

I offer an invocation,

To her,

To you:

I will not tame you.

I will not be tamed.

May your wildness stay

Be it here,

Or away.

Life is so Blessed

Life is so blessed with your life
  In Presence
    With your Years Lived wisely
    In newness and Joy

Pure is your Soul-call to life
  Deep longings
    Responding each moment
    Authentic and true

Destiny knocks and you respond
  Powerful passion
    Glee and gratitude
    Your hearts' calling card

A legacy of one life - not yet even
  Half-journeyed
    In life's resonant breath
    Walked strong, hand-in-hand

Witnessing Your Journey
  Stepping gently,
    In awe of each moment
    With two beating hearts

I love you and honour
  Your beauty and presence
    The power and the brilliance
    That is you – only you

Anchor Points

Grief mixes with uncertainty.

Is she gone for good?

Will she return?

Time passes…

Yet the gap remains.

Roam new ground.

Feel grief

Disorientation

Fear and separation

Containment

Sound the call for release:

Freedom.

Aloneness

Oneness

All oneness

New lands in a known landscape

New anchor points found

Safe togetherness ground

Relationships profound

Companionship

Love

Loyalty

The constant weave.

The Ants and the Pistachio Nut

One ant cannot move a nut larger than itself.
It's simply too big,
Too insurmountable,
Out of the question.
So they don't.

Even though
They try.

That's why they do it together,
Circle up with others
To tend the task,
Shift the stash
Into the depths.

In service of
the whole.

Maybe we should learn from the ants.
Circle up together
To tend the tasks
That are too big
For one.

Together
We move mountains.

Sunsets and New Horizons

In twenty-four hours
I witnessed both.
Facing east, west and south,
In one breath life shifted,
Uplifted,
Into the new.

Darkness, light, shadows,
Bright,
All in one day.
Horizons mark the edge
Where transits are seen.

In one breath life weaved,
Believed,
Into the new.

It's all present, effervescent,
All in one day.

We know the Circle

Human beings,
Ones of nature,
We know the circle.

Presence names it,
Centre created,
We know the circle.

Disturbance strikes,
Calls for wisdom,
We create the circle.

Abundant beauty,
Shaped with magic,
We birth the circle.

Blessèd wholeness,
Wild creation,
Life's a Circle.

The Stairway

Stairway created
Rising upwards
To
The next level

Open vistas
Panoramas
Far
Distant horizons

Breathing deeply
Shaping further
New
Possibilities

Economy's Claim

How was I reduced
To the perspective of money
When my original calling was
To keep order at home?

Mutuality, reciprocity,
Exchange and hard cash.
This wide blessèd bounty,
Inspired and intended.

The pendulum must swing
From scarcity to abundance,
Reclaiming the pattern,
Roots to high purpose.

Economy's debtors,
Chalked up over time
Claim come and repattern
Re-member to home's hearth.

What's your Practice? Practice it!

When all around feels so unclear,
What's your practice?
Practice it!

When all within is chased by fear,
What's your practice?
Practice it!

When truth seems very hard to find,
What's your practice?
Practice it!

When life feels like a daily grind,
What's your practice?
Practice it!

When love is free but never here,
What's your practice?
Practice it!

When all that's wished is really near,
What's your practice?
Practice it!

When maps are old and times are new,
What's your practice?
Practice it!

When Life says Hey, I'm calling you,
What's your practice?
Practice it!

Death and the New Dawn

Death came a-knocking
When all seemed quite perfect,
Sloughing off edges
With precision
Of a surgeon's knife,
Cutting to the core
Until soul was wide open,
Exposed to bright sunlight
Heart's beating, sore.

It's time!
I'm not ready.
Wrong! It's time!
I won't go.
All is well
Who says so?
You, Him, Her,
Not me!

Yet deep in her bones
She knew that it was time
A lump rising strongly,
Tightening her throat.
In crashed the waves
Of grief and not-knowing,

Breaking the mold
Crafted in years.

Dreams shed, light glimmers
With night-times' soft gaze,
Metaphor sung lullabies,
Soothing soul's craze.
Decipher us dreams spoke,
Night after night-time,
Confusing and clear signs
Lighting pathways.

Seals, dolphins, edges,
Trilogies, women's circles,
Gatherings and journeys,
Decapitated homes.
Messages spoke loudly
Into the dreamtime,
Butterflies in daylight
Beckoning the move.

To distant horizons,
No clearer, no nearer.
Then Death boomed *No further*
One morning: *That's it.*

With a firm hand he held high,
Once again: It is now.
Head bowed with reverence,
The only response.

Timing held knowing,
The resistance was over,
Time to go edgy
Where known meets the void.
Searing pain circled,
Breathing fire through the vortex,
Burning holes, burning off
Any remnant or claim.

Response was to trust now
To life's gracious cycles,
A phase was now over
A new one lived soon.
In one moment, acceptance,
Held palms facing upwards,
Tense shoulders eased downwards,
As grace drank full tears.

Death had been honoured
As one of life's seer's,

The strength to be present
Signalling deep shifts.
A guardian of thresholds
Bringing insights and blessings
That life from this moment
Will never be the same.

Void waited with silence
Alongside her master
Present for ages
Gone in a glimpse.
Void too was honoured
With truth, as all others,
Blessed with full presence
To boldly move on.

Beyond death was newness,
Dawn lit up in brilliance,
Birthing a new day
Blessed by the rains.
Rewarded with magic,
The scent of new landscapes,
Filled with possibility:
It's time, come and play.

Truth took Life's Next Step

Paradox stretched, boldly holding
Newness and Knowing,
Tensioning the tightrope
For Consciousness to step.

With lightness of footing,
Choice chose to not choose,
Outcome fell silent
And Space remained clear.

Centre stayed open
As Options drew nearer,
Breathing in Newness
With possibilities abound.

Yet just at the edge
Action became edgy,
Pressing for Clarity
To raise her hand high.

But Trust slid in closer,
The bridger of answers,
Steadying Not Knowing,
Craving to speak.

Wisdom stayed steady
Until Timing was ready,
Sensing that evolution
Had paced all landscapes.

Source drew Depth nearer
As Wisdom was ripened,
Threshold the truth-speaker
Readying the word.

Tuning Fork quivered,
Alignment breathed deeply.
Truth took life's next step
Followed by all.

Rain Drops' Joy

Rain drop awakened,
Renewed from his sleeping,
Yawning and stretching
From deep in the clouds.

Travelling for aeons
In cycles of timing,
Climbing high heavenward,
Descending in waves.

Life had clear purpose:
Cleanse earthen-dry landscapes,
Birth all the newness,
Fill up the wells.

Rain's joy was in downpours,
Mates from the dew clan,

Swarming formations,
Drenching all ways.

Wild was his passion,
Yet stopping for moments
To rest on a tree branch,
Spider's web or a leaf.

Power to move mountains,
Forge caves over lifetimes,
Bless buds time of
blooming,
Quench our thirst as well.

Celebrate rain's gifting,
Offers and deep service.
He's a trickster I grant you,
He shifts roads as well!

Doorways

'When one door closes
Another door opens;
But we so often look so long
And so regretfully upon the closed door,
That we do not see the ones
Which open for us.'

Alexander Graham Bell

When one door opens,
Another door closes;
But we so often look so long
And so hopefully upon the open door,
That we do not see the ones
Which close for us.

When one door opens,
Another door opens;
But we so often look so long
And so definitively upon the doorways,
That we do not see the ones
Which journey with us.

Metamorphosis

Since the time
For humanity
To ground
The new
Consciousness
On Earth
Is here,

Void tends

The endings
At the doorways:
Glimpsed, retraced,
Faced, embraced,
Let go.

Grieving,

Slowly
Breathing
Into
The
Presence
Of
The new.

Occupy's Call

Occupy's heart beats
Soul's street
Calls to life:
Keep shining bright
In eyes
That see the now.

Occupy's love light
Delight's height
Share the feeling
Keep believing
That all is
Truly one.

Occupy pure breath
Immense depth
Hold the centre
Truth connector
Blessing life
With life.

Occupy deep pain
Sheering shame
Light the shadow
Feel the bardo
Conscience
Rebalancing:

Occupy.

Return the Pane

Birth day banner
Ceremony's honour
At the cradle

Elbow raising
Shudders glazing
Glass is broken

Lock twists
A key exists
Blocking entry

Life's shatter
Helper's clatter
Spread is gathered

Circle gift
A woman slips
Over thresholds

Cutting newness
Family business
Pane's created

Returning home
State unknown
Climbing skyward

Five months later
Winter's painter
Opens timing

Minds bend
Hands depend
The system musters

Glazier's placing
Scratch blood's raising
Nails knocked inwards

Seeing answers
Trouble tampers
Within the hour

Firelights glimmer
Hearth's red shimmer
Heat returning

Sing Tones of the Sea Tides

Initiate the opening,
Bumblebee the breeze,
Bless baptismal seashores,
Landscape frames retrieved.

Sing tones of the sea tides,
Initiate the way,
Hear voices now awakened,
Life song within each day.

Pour grace along the shorelines,
See soulmates hold the edge,
It's time for the reunions,
With instincts pulse our pledge.

Dig out all that's latent,
Bleed out all the pain,
Strip to what is needed,
Dive in deep, unashamed.

Challenge life to show you
In every single breath,
Call in love's great knowing,
So Earth is truly met.

Soul Stretches

Dust gathered day by day

Month by month

Until suddenly seeing

Clutter and debris

Hoarded items

Left untended.

Time to spring clean

Psyche's environs

Shrouded layers

Dormant, untended

Inhabitants expelled

Vanquished.

Soul stretches

Psyche whispers

Touch me again

Tend me with candlelight

Music and ceremony

Love. Sweet life.

Humanity's Change

Of all the people
I met today,

In the post office
The town telephone office
The city telephone office
The shops
The street
The supermarket
The hypermarket,

Only one person
Smiled in return.

A man in his seventies,
Standing at the traffic lights
Holding an empty cup
Asking for change
From people driving by.

I held out my hand
Before he asked me
To offer change
And I smiled.
He met my gaze
And smiled in return
He walked to my car
And received the change

Into his cup.

I blessed his day,
He blessed my day in return.

What change do we truly need?
More smiles in one day,

More generosity from the heart,
More compassion,
More presence.

Perhaps this is the change of
Grace for humanity
At this time of great change.

Ode to Transformation

We may believe we know
Who transformation is,
But until we meet
And embrace her fully:

Head first
Feet first
Soul First
Heart First,

We cannot even perceive
The dissolution required,
The waves that result,
Crashing through the cracks

Of our known existence,
Carving through stone,
Breaking old ground,
Ill-equipped to host the new.

Life sears through time,
Trembling the edges of soul
Dying to break out
Into new consciousness.

Whistling through corridors
Patrolled with demons
The gatekeepers
Holding too tight.

Blow them out!
It's time.
Let go.

Birth yourself,
And your newness,
Walk step by step,

Climb the stairway
To destiny's chambers,
Breathe the fresh air.

Feel it coursing,
Coercing
Every cell

Until the dawn
Warms the day
Of the new world

Waiting just beyond
The Seeing,
The Believing.

Trust life's hand,
Re-patterning within
And without.

Move:
Do not stand too long
On the edge,

Lean out,
Feel the rope holding
The tensions of time,

Bless goodness,
Pathways and memories,
Let the love live on.

⌒

The tide
Turns

The path
Shifts

The new
Opens

The soul
Awakens

Constellations
Shaken
Life
Is lived

⌒

Whole-heartedly
Wild-naturedly
Soul-connectedly

⌒

Fully.

Cracked Open

The nerve vibrates,
Struck like a spider thread
Spun throughout time.

The soul echoes,
Responding to the touch,
Hidden, yet revealing.

Distant clouds billow storms
Balancing the edge
Of night-time and day.

Tumultuous downpour,
Lightening strikes sun-soaked Earth
Cracked open in dissolution.

⌣⟶

The ground shakes
Struck by the giants of old
Turning in their beds.

The Earth echoes
Trembling to the touch,
Fearful, yet believing.

Distant memories quiver,
Consciousness balancing the edge
Of night-time and day.

Tumultuous tremors
Crashing across sun-soaked Earth
Cracked open in transformation.

⌣⟶

The heart breaks
Struck by life's universal,
Limitless love.

The breath echoes,
Gasping to the touch,
Holding, yet surrendering.

Distant beings assemble,
Nurturance balancing the edge
Of night-time and day.

Tumultuous tending
Races across sun-soaked Earth
Cracked open in brilliance.

The structures quakes,
Struck by the knowing
That destiny is here.

The spirit rises,
Breathtaking to the touch,
Prayerful, yet revering.

Parallel light-lines crescendo,
Insight balancing the edge
Of night-time and day.

Tumultuous timing awakening,
Sun-soaked Earth cracked,
Opening to home.

Beat Loud This Day

One, two, three,
Keeping you alive
You see,

Without the heart,
The soul won't start
To make its mark,

It's the law
We are here for
The best call

Called life
Waking us every day
To say our best yes,

The one that may
Redress all that makes
Our hearts feel low.

But I know
That when the beat is on
The song is strong,

Listen to your heart
When you really have
Something to say.

It's loud!
Beating wide and proud
To wake you, make you

Show what you truly care
for.

So beat loud this day
As the beat of life
Beats on.

www.ingramcontent.com/pod-product-compliance
Lightning Source LLC
Chambersburg PA
CBHW061458040426
42450CB00008B/1410